TEAR DROPS OF FALLEN ANGELS

ANTHONY HUGHES

DEDICATION

This book is dedicated to my mother Ms. Bernita Ann Ward and my late father Mr. Anthony Hughes, Sr., without their hard work and dedication to my survival I would not be here to provide you with these words.

This book also is dedicated to all my brothers and sisters fighting through this thing we call life. A special dedication to all those who did not make it through thus far in the physical form.

Contents

Acknowledgement

Some refer to America as the land of the free; while others believe that this is the land of opportunity. Despite the images many individuals have created in their minds about the world's most powerful nation; reality tells us the truth—America is not free of its old age custom of discrimination. Racism is a disease that plagues society and destroys the very fabric of any relations that can be established amongst ethnic groups residing in the same region. By studying the history of this nation, one can find the root to the problems that have derailed the progress of many ethnic groups. It is true that over time things do change, but the course taken to right the mistakes of the past must be implemented with a moral and ethical approach. Only then will we truly see a change in the way we view one another as human beings--without a person's color, nationality, religious preference, gender, age, sexuality or ethnicity hampering our decision of embracing them as a brother at the table of humanity.

The prejudice attitude of many throughout the world has done harm to the character of those who they have discriminated against. Wars have been waged because of prejudice feelings of one group towards another. Additionally, various ethnic groups in America have not been fully welcomed into all sectors of society because of preconceived thoughts about their character and ability.

A Rampage of Broken Dreams

A rampage of broken dreams along with hopeless thoughts have trapped and captured my soul. Brothers and sisters, the end is near and as I shed a tear, the fears that reside within have been washed away. I pray to the One above and ask that He keep me in His graces. Soldier, I have changed more than once and still hunt for my identity. My life is my broken dream and the blood that flows through my veins has developed the rampage within me.

I use the mirror to reflect back on my life, but the vision I receive is unclear. I've done things backwards and forward but nothing positive has ever come from it. I'm knee deep in the game of life flirting with my third strike. Damn, it is hard to continue even though my world, to an extent, has been destroyed. I catch glimpses of the life I envisioned myself living, even though it has and probably will never come to past.

Laughter replaces my true feelings about my situation. I was taught that one must find some humor in everything, smile when things are tough so no one really knows your true feelings. Only a few actually understand the real me because they genuinely care. I find it hard to separate those who are sincere from those who are fake, so I tend to run from everyone. By running, I hurt those who care, while I rid myself of those who have latched onto me for the ride. I think it is time to stop hiding now as I allow myself the freedom to feel again. I am a man who is unworthy of the love that has been pushed in my direction by so many. However, the time has come for me to end my dance with the devil because we have walked side by side for so many years. I don't regret our time together for the simple reason that the being who calls the shots allowed me to walk that path. Until the path in front of me is clear, the rampage within me will continue to shatter my dreams.

(This particular piece is an attempt to capture the hurt one feels as they look to the future for answers that have eluded them in the past.)

The Covenant Amongst Men

The love amongst men must be strong and unbreakable. Yes, unbreakable nothing should come in between their ties as brothers. Casual conversations lead to deeper intellectual debates. Men must strive to be great in their own right, but a team that strives for greatness can control their world. Covenants are not made to be broken but strengthened by the love of those that have committed themselves to each other. Passionate dealings are all that we have to look forward to because misfortunes are present in the world. Lay your life on the table to be sacrificed in the event that your brother is in need. Breathe the same air as your fellow soldier.

Break bread with him whether he is in need of a meal or just for the simple fact that it is suppertime. Brandish the sword of war when he is confronted with danger. Ask the same of him because we treat one another with the respect worthy of men. (I must always keep my brothers in mind when I come across something that will benefit us as a group). Never dishonor each other by speaking out against one another to others outside of the covenant. Secrets are to be carried to the grave and rest there for eternity. Blessed are those who show interest in the lives of those they love. Bare my pain and develop a cure for my heartache. Brother, you are my existence as your family is also my family. These ties we have created may never be severed. Our journey has just begun and more trials will come to test our faith in one another.

Never Bend

Dangerous encounters hurt those involved because violence is a route to death. Death unleashes the soul but can destroy the lives of those close to the person who has passed. Tainted vessels we are but the message is scrambled within us all. The craziness of our lives hides the true feelings of the ghetto dwellers. I am trying to free my mind and unwind in the present year. As the future hits the corner, I have no idea what my thoughts will be because I do not hold the answer to that mystery, but to bend and surrender is one thing I will never do. Even if all the stones are stacked in the other corner, I will charge on into the fray with sword and gun in hand.

Never will I or anyone who I consider a comrade relinquish their position. The dark tunnel through which I travel provides patches of light. If I can break free and run to the light without anyone grabbing at my feet, not even my master will be able to stop my escape. I am a man of courage and valor. Apathy spells out my approach towards dealing with others outside of my electrical field. I find myself constantly drilling in holes that are already tapped out, dreaming of the past, and, looking forward to the future as I wonder what it holds for me.

Moral law will provide the structure for my people to follow so that we can be in conscience with the ruler. Daytime arises as the earth rotates on its imaginary axis. I have no baggage because the open chapters of my life are closed and sealed not to be revisited again.

The Comrades' Party

Single-family homes dominate the lives of my guys. Either lost to death or lost to society, the fathers were gone; left behind were the young squarers. They left us alone to grow into the men you see before you today. Mothers could not show us how to be men so uncles, older cousins, brothers, and grandfathers tried to fill the void created by the separation of the boy from his father. Still that was not enough. Once we found each other, there would be no separation of the group of boys brought together by the bonds we created through the love that we shared over the years. The sensation of all night smoke sessions, along with drinking, at the tender age of fourteen was our passion because it helped kill the pains we suffered at an early age.

The destruction of our pain was the obstacle we were trying to destroy so that we could move on and accomplish the goals we had set for ourselves. Nothing got in the way of our continuous party. Not even the death of a loved one. It was only a matter of years that we came to the conclusion that life is not promised. The lust of money, drugs and love were our additions. Women were a distant fourth; "MOB" was the call when things would get out of perspective. That call made things seem so clear. "You need money, fuck them bitches" was our motto.

We learned at a young age that women at this stage in life were accessories, not tangible things. Love is that illusion that keeps men grounded, and, hinders their flight into prosperity. Personally, I would rather get high than pursue the pie in a flower dress. The quest during the early years was to be the highest of the high and the freshest of the fresh. Doing things niggas our age could only dream of.

The team brought together by the souls that we posses, never settled for less. It was "give me it all or I don't want it at all." We were so close that it seems as though we were one. We tried hard not to let anyone fall too far off because the ties we share are closer than blood. When one hurt, we all hurt, and, if God permits, we will go to the end of the world to bring each other back.

Nowadays, we may be apart so that we can accomplish what must be done to better ourselves as individuals. The acquisition of degrees and money are put in motion to secure our everlasting party. The task has changed because we are constantly developing our minds. We do not view the world the same, but we still struggle with our past demons no matter what we do to push them aside. Yet, we hide from no one, and we present ourselves in a manner that frightens the weak and gains respect from the strong.

We are holding on and waiting for our time, but we are taking steps to push ourselves into positions where we will not have to wait. The collaboration of our minds along with ideas will relinquish upon this world a jewel it has never seen before. We have evolved in our thinking and are still on that evolutionary track of developing our minds into lethal weapons. You must face us for we will make you hear us and feel our pains. Life has shown us the way...believe it, we are here to stay.

The Development of a Lost World

Terror destroys the lives of the lost souls who are unable to battle with the scary sites of street life, don't fold. It's cold down here in the pits of hell but I run well in between the two worlds that create my cell. Followers tell stories of those they aspire to be but not me. I am free to see the light from the eyes of the Lord. The sword protects the head of the Highlander whose only mission is to be the last man standing. I trample those in the way laying a path of destruction that leads to the reconstruction of the world I have destroyed. Laugh no more for I hold the keys to your existence in hand. The majority of the time I find it hard to hold men in high regard. The circle is falling apart amongst those who pledged their allegiance to one another. My comrades, don't you see the end coming to the game we have played for so many years? It is time to move on and develop a new scheme while leaving the game behind altogether. My most loyal and respected friends have joined me in my quest to form a plan that will produce longevity. I believe the time has come to set aside our differences and grasp the light of power as we share that power equally amongst ourselves.

Thoughts in the Mind of an Educated Street Nigga

The passionate dream of being free drives me to the point of craziness. I am free within my mind but my physical presence is stuck in a state of bondage. I take to the street to obtain a state of economic freedom, which I think will free me from my captivity but in all reality it is leading to the trapping of my mind. The inner battle taking place in my mind drives me insane. Even though I am a child born into a family of well off people, who go without to secure a future for me, I want more.

My greed is natural because I am human. Better yet, I am a human who is given the description of being black when my skin is brown. I believe my bondage has to do with the institution, which has been installed to hold back the true princes of this world called earth. My struggle to have what I feel I deserve tears apart the fibers of life. The feeling rips through my tissue and embeds deep within the core of my heart. I am a troubled soul torn in two directions, what society thinks is righteous, and, what my heart tells me is right. After all, society has draped its hands around my body and squeezed until the juices are nearly gone.

The strongest of men are prone to be exploited by the society that built them up to be great. The hate that fuels my soul holds back my ascent into the higher echelons of life. Strike the dinner bell, it is time to sit at the table and break the bread for supper. My piece of bread is getting smaller everyday; the dinner bell has rung and supper is served. This leaves me no alternative but to turn my back on those who mistreat me when it is time to give out the portions for survival. War is waging. This drive I posses for life ignites my motives to gain more than I have by any means I deem necessary.

Danger within My Mind

The danger that is present is overwhelming at times for my mind to comprehend. It gets harder and harder as time passes to separate love, respect, and envy because men can mask these emotions easily. The cancer that goes by the name of society can destroy my mind, my drive for life and my ambition. In these days for my own sanity I will distance myself from the riggers of civilization. Socializing with my fellow man can be dangerous because the majority is blinded by the illusions that are put in front of them.

To be myself and interact with others places me in jeopardy, because this society has always destroyed what it fears. My inner circle of close-knit friends is the last resort for me. This is the last line of communication for me because of the proven love we have shown one another. The rest of the aristocracies receive the mask, which I present to them so that I can prosper until I can vanish out of sight and mind.

I might retire to a cave or a secluded island, but wherever it may be, it will be far away from the masses. At times, this society makes me sick to the point I want to destroy its comfort zone and introduce it back to the time before civilization. The land in which I live has proven to be the master of deception. Do you not understand that the same time they move on others it moves on you? Pay attention! This country justifies everything it does by using the media to mask its image. Who do you think supplies the uprisings in these countries abroad to solidify its power? I have to shut up because I can be silenced if this message moves too many.

Hello Father

If heaven was within arm's length,

I would never come back to hell after climbing
into the cradle of true love.

Receive me Lord for the man that I am;

I know there is no limitation on the number to
be admitted.

Drown my sins in poison.

Breathe into this temple life again.

Now move out of my way so that I can blossom
into a god, too.

I believe there is room for another like you.

Maybe there is room for another whose powers
dwarf yours

You never said there weren't other gods. You
simply stated that we should not put no other god
before thee.

What if you don't meet my needs?

Can't I find one that suits my agenda?

I believe so.

Free will, right!

Out of Favor

Constantly falling out of grace with the one
being that truly loves us all

Lost in the wilderness of shadows and dreams

Never fraternize with the enemy for the simple
fact that evil will do one in

Silence rings in the ear but fear holds the higher
note

Caught by the rope of hate

Hesitation evaporates trust

That trust in turn returns in raindrops of lust

Blossoming flowers are dead within a day of
bloom

Have I chosen this path or has the path of the
unlawful chosen me

Noble deeds are committed for desire

Can I hire men who fumble their lives as I

Atrocities bleed buckets of guilt

I am an angel with demon attributes

The world is the battleground

My vital principle is the war

Amun, place me back under your light, I can't take it no more, save me tonight.

The Changing Truth

I question all that is told to me by man regardless of the proof that they present to back up their thoughts. Times and days change as though there is a revolving door which manifest a different truth. The positive attributes of those thoughts that have troubled mine have put my energy in an endless search for the truth. Can I have an empty feeling even though I am full of knowledge? Regardless of the amount of information present within my mind there is always room for more. As I walk among my peers, I take time out to ask the questions others are afraid to ask. The heavens are calling and I am answering their call. Mythical and religious stories bare the same structure, which reveals to me that the writers of those texts have influenced each other. The story of Ra and Genesis are one within the same. I cannot carry the sins of my brothers but I can come to grips with my own. Please listen to the pain in my writing and understand that it comes from the heart. Even though I have been blessed with overwhelming guidance from those who have been placed in my circle, I am cursed by my very existence and what I represent. I represent a people who have been dealt a bad hand and judged by thoughts that have been concocted to stop us from prospering in this land.

Strategic Thinking

Thoughts run through my mind in the sequence resembling that of a war plan. These thoughts are well scripted and carefully planned out to the T, but no plan is without flaws because no thought is actually complete. The movements within my mind simulate the strategies of chess, checks and balances. The plan is not just a military scheme or a scientific method; it consists of all the righteous and wicked plots I can conceive to free myself from the chains of oppression. Like that of the closed minds of older individuals who more regularly control the direction in which society moves. Set yourself free and open your minds to newer philosophies, so that the achievements or goals of the younger generations are met.

The development of the mind is a magnificent prize for any man and should be held in high regard. I will never forget the goals of my predecessors and their achievements. The lesson was well taught and I will show the world that the lesson was well learned.

In memory of all the slain and prosecuted speakers of the truth, your thoughts and legacies live on in us - the new regime of intellects and warriors.

At Rest at an Early Age

In my quest to hold what is most precious in mind, the troublesome thought of surviving blinds my vision. The devastation places my soul at rest at an early age. The gage of our lives in the communities that breed the desperation of all souls holds no single danger zone because the community itself is a danger zone. Shouldn't we all be able to experience the life we envisioned for ourselves? The worldwide massacre of people was present in the 20th century and is an active agent in the minds of men in the 21st century.

Dedication is the key to the unprecedented change of the guard. The movement of people in the classes of society will be no more. Equality will actually be achieved for the people who walk this earth. I believe this thought is a plea to the Most High to stop the pain of His children who have come to understand about the wrong we have done. Please release us from bondage. Release our spirits, show us the way back to prosperity.

An Endless Quest for Freedom

Flashbacks of images and past events are rampant in the mind of a man who searches for the final answers to the puzzle of life. Life is a cluster of events and memories that shape the souls men. So, the thought of another man placing limitations on my life ignites my soul with fire. The fire that burns within my interior is the result of the external use of my hands along with my mind to do battle with oppressors who plot to confine me to a cage and kill my free spirit. Oppressors hold no special color. They are present in all walks of life. At times, your own kind can do more to hold you back than others. Remove the shades from your eyes. The sun is tucked away. Experience some of the attributes of the gray area. Nothing is concrete and everything is debatable. One can establish different ideologies and except more than one truth about a particular subject. Awake from the slumber of the ignorant and think for yourselves. Stop taking the easy way out by allowing others to set the tone for you. Be individuals, not puppets with strings attached to their back for the puppet master to pull. High is He, high as thee, highest of the souls to be me. I am an individual, free to think and live my life as I see fit. Followers are not allowed in the circle because the circle consists of no one but me. I am not your soldier nor am I your sheep to be led off into slaughter. In the words of a former president twisted to suit my situation "ask not what you can do for your country but what your country can do for you." My platform is unmovable because my thoughts are cemented in my mind. I curse those who will try to force upon me what they want me to believe. I will say to them for the final time, leave me alone because my anger knows no bounds.

The Lonely Voyage

Leave me to be lonely and happy by myself.

Stop coming around to see if I'm okay.

I pace back and forth, up and down the house
looking for my identity;

I have not yet found it.

Bet me that I never will,

I bet that I won't either.

Because I am digging too deep into a soul that is
a bottomless pit

Stripped of its guts and killed by its luck.

Runaway, as I tell you to do when you see me
enter the room. I bring trickery and deceit to the
table.

Never follow my path young man,

I drive people to come into my realm of
thinking.

I am a product of my society,

Better yet I am a product of the nation of liberty
and justice for all.

When I fall I will not rise to take my place in the
sky with the gods.

I will reside in the underworld with the other
lost souls.

Even though I will not rise, I have never
relinquished my position in my eyes.

A Breath

Oh, a breath

To inhale and exhale is a blessing.

Yes, to be able to breathe again clearly without
the fumes and pollution surrounding me.

I breathe the same air as my fellow man but long
for a breath of fresh air.

Announce that I am free to be uneven.

Devilish thoughts hold deviant minds in awe,

Vacant hideouts are a plus for those who move
in stealth.

Bring me the grail so that I can drink from the
cup of eternal life.

Hide my appearance with costumes that leave
no trace of who I am

As I bend down to kiss the feet of my father,

He places his hands upon my head to raise me
to eye level.

He whispers in my ear

Don't worry son the only air here is pure and
undisturbed.

Open Your Eyes and See

The misinterpretation or redirection of our education can be contributed to our relocation to a new land along with the European expansion of the 15th century. We once had our own philosophies and our own way of doing things. We have allowed ourselves to be steered in a direction that does not suit our situation because we were too weak to say no and right our own mistakes. After looking deeper into the problems that have manifested themselves; I have come to understand that we are still slaves. I, mean, our minds are still controlled by those that control the world, but we are not the only people who are suffering from this misfortune. The giant beast in the west is and will always try to make others conform to their way of life. The United States of America enforces its will on whomever they want regardless if the people in question oppose their control. The U.S. government uses money-hungry leaders to make the people of different nations submit and relinquish their wealth into the hands of bureaucrats who use that wealth to start wars and fuel the U.S. propaganda tool. I am a native of this country and speak out against it because I am not a citizen who is recognized with the same presence of others when the laws were first written. Who would know better than my people not to trust the promises made to the public by these congressmen who have no intention on following through with them. I don't understand why foreigners believe this is the land of freedom and democracy. One hand washes the other and one wrong justifies another. This is the motto of many governments that have conspired against the people that they are suppose to serve. The signs are clear and my eyes are open wide. Brothers and sisters of all nationalities and creeds wake up from your slumber. The trap has been set and the plan of global control is in progress. No one will be able to save you but yourselves.

Stars and Stripes Burn Tonight

The flag, which some Americans hold so dear, will be burned tonight, not by fire, but in the minds of many around the world. The thoughts of a free nation are no longer the focus of their minds. Their focus is now set on destroying the country which keeps them grounded by its false promises and its use of corrupt foreign policies to destroy economies abroad. Dreams of tearing this country to pieces are present in the minds of many. Conspirators are planning the fall of America within the walls of its infrastructure. Those who plot against the American way of life are learning the customs, absorbing the thoughts of its people, discovering its weaknesses and waiting for their turn to unleash a plague on the American society. The oceans that once kept this country from its enemies are no longer a big obstacle. America is scared of what might be her last stand. Her last attempt to hold on to the power she has grown so accustom to having at her disposal.

This country is driven by the hard work and blood of people who have no say in the events that take place. The young see the misuse of funds that lead to the enrichment of government officials' pockets. I say burn bitch, burn and allow for a reversal of the governmental structure. America understands why I feel this way. How can't they? Past injustices are present in everyday life. Look up, down, to the right and to the left. You don't have to break your neck to point out segregation within the cities, schools, communities, health facilities, and exedra.

In memory of the Panthers, Malcolm X, and others who believe revolution is a war that consists of blood shed and the conquest of land.

Life, Justice, and Liberty for All

This statement rings in the ears of people throughout the world. The sense of freedom, which eludes the masses, grabs my attention because I am a fighter of oppression at all levels. The guidance I have received from my respected teachers has not limited my education but opened my eyes to a world of new thoughts, philosophies which shape the minds of men in our modern day and time. I reach out and grasp those monumental achievements of these great philosophers and hone my own philosophical thought. The pressure is now here but the masterful malnutrition of the mind is no longer the obstacle of my circle. The influx of information is the only agenda on my table. The cable has been cut that links my mind to the destruction of itself. Please help us achieve life, justice, and liberty because this thought has been one of mistrust. Sign here, here, and here, show no fear for we will reject an institution that does not resemble us in character and nature. This irresponsible act of tricking the public into believing the government holds your best interest at heart has come in many forms during the time of this world's existence. The conspirators of the world come together to deny us that very thought. The hope is gone. The movement has moved on to a new agenda. The prosperity of a nation of people equal in all the same ways. That terminology to me is misconstrued and an irresponsible thought to have when we must move swiftly to achieve the goal of respectability. The latter is the measure at hand and should be conscious in the minds of all men whether wealthy or poor. The fruits of labor my dear neighbor leave us with nothing but broken spirits drained of our youth and strength, turn that labor into private business so that we can achieve the goal of life, justice, and liberty for all.

Life Unravels

The purpose of my life will not materialize until I am dead and gone. The rope around my neck is getting tighter as Osiris pulls on the cord attached to his hand. If I go before the next sunrise place pennies on my eyes so that I can pay for my passage into the next world. Without any regrets, I will enter into the next stage of life. All I ask is that my family is well off. I cannot depart from this world without my mind being at peace with my soul. Taking the road of the misfortunate has made me more appreciative of those who love me for me and not what I can do for them. I am dedicated to the war present in the society in which I live. My war is an internal one geared in the direction of self-fulfillment. Unfortunately, I am empty at this stage in my life. Dark voids fill many areas that make a whole individual ready for his or her voyage into the realm of the Most High. Hurting myself leads to the annihilation of my character. What replaces my character is the work of evil forces that engulf my essence. My power is dwarfed by this magnificent presence. I must come to grips with the demons inside me to right my path before I set out to help others. Can I nurture myself and allow nature to take its course? I don't know but I think I am going to give it a chance, because my power is fading and I need a new source to draw from to stay alive in this grieved stricken world. May the sun shine on me and those that the Lord favors for eternity.

Conjuring Death

Crowed surroundings clutter the mind

The different styles of dress and the unique
smells of perfumes turn the stomach

People are everywhere, no room to breathe

No room to hide from your enemy

Predators lurk amongst their prey

Hell is here for us to take advantage of

Strong arm the population one wishes to control

Systematic killing rings in the ears of those men
who thirst for blood

Leave no stone unturned when in search of
hope

Hope to some is in the form of dope

Drugs alleviate the memories of pain but after
the effect of the drug wears off

The memories of those painful events reappear
with deadlier thoughts

Thoughts haunt the soul

The soul loses the fight with the mind

Next, the body rejects the mind and the soul

Finally, men fold and die the deaths they have conjured up for themselves.

The Victim's Plea

Once, again, I have fallen victim to the society which has developed me. I am trapped in a never-ending cycle full of hate and resentment of who I am. The cleverness of the ethnic group who has made me feel this way is overbearing at times. Through these eyes, I have seen men who look like me meet their demise over and over again. After looking into the mirror I see a face that holds a story. The story has its good moments along with the bad, but the bad moments stand out more because of the scars present on the face. My battle marks run deep because my compassion for the next man's feelings is infinite. The staggering difference in others and me is that I have to hold in a lot of what I feel. The reason for the bottling of my feelings is that I cannot express them without showing weakness. Weakness can lead to the ultimate undoing of a person. The removal of his or her drive to stay alive can destroy them in a matter of a moment. I have to stay strong and remain brave as I walk along the path that is constructed beneath my feet. The time has come for me to look into the eyes of men and say unto them all please do not be an instrument in my downfall.

A Soldier in Search of the Emperor's Position

The life that men lead will materialize in their eyes. It is idiotic to hide from the truth and run into the dark blind. Disturb the villages as we plunder them and take the spoils for the comrades. Towering minds are what we posses. The conquests of others' thoughts along with their possessions are in the line of fire. I am the voyager awaiting my orders. The ruler is not sure what the next move should be to solidify his power. While he is wondering in his mind, I am developing a nation of my own to oppose his. I might be a soldier but I posses the soul and mind of a conqueror. Even though I have manipulated my way into his heart, he has left me no choice in the matter because he has become stagnant. Within my brain, the circuitry works at a continuous pace, never is there a break in my thought process. My sleep haunts my mind with ideas of conquest. Rivals are what we have become in this day and age. I trained his army and appointed all of his generals to their post for the simple reason that those generals are weak. As time passes and war is waged between us, my former ruler has been placed under my command because of his indecisive nature. I consider all the situations of war, and, pay close attention to the ways of man. My queen is my go between; she flirts and talks to other kings giving them the impression that she has fallen out of favor with my regime. The campaign is now complete and another nation has been placed under my control. To free myself from the feeling of sympathy for my fellow man, I will start a new campaign to bring all my people together under one sign. The sign in question is the sign of love.

Relieve me of My Pain

Wash away my pain in a green shaped bottle

Gather the remains and spread them throughout
the four corners of the world.

The thrill of breaking bread with the disciples
grasps my heart and places it in a wringer.

Am I awake or am I still dreaming;

Demons awake me, can the Lord save me? I
don't know.

The Conscious of an Ambitious Man

My world has been French kissed

Dismissed for reasons unknown

Read from the mouth of pain

No shame but fame is in my reach

At last the moment has come

I don't know if I'm willing to go forth with the
devilish act

The bell has rung

The time has come to an end

I must take your life my dearest friend.

Time to Move On

The damage has been done and the crime has been committed, but I am still here to spread the truth because I am the speaker of the truth. Stand up and become the man I am destined to become. The time has come to take a stand and no longer run from the troubles that break my spirit. Pass over the rainbow and enter into the alternative world full of love, not the hate that is the glimmer of the dead, in this world. I have come to the realization that I am tied to nothing but part of everything. The reconstruction of what has been destroyed is my mission whether it is physical or supernatural. The sky is gray for the moment but it will return to a shade of blue once the people are set free to view the heavens without anyone tampering with their eyes.

Endless Possibilities

Life promises nothing but offers an endless amount of opportunities for those who are willing to pursue a goal. Leave those who are not ready to join the regime leery with no hope of joining us in our succession from the blind. Remind me of the reasons I have taken the game of life seriously. As my fellow brothers and I converse send someone into our circle that can further educate us on issues that we have not been able to master. The gathering has begun and we must hold the information passed between us in high regard. The messages of other regimes have conspired against the public in order to hoard their belongings. Worldwide conquest has rung in the ears of men for eternity. Our responsibility to the public is nothing because we rule by divine right. God did not give that right to us in order to reign over our fellow man. We have chosen to take it upon ourselves to appoint those we feel will further the regimes cause to office. Diplomacy is a must but our objectives will be met even if it requires force. We are after everything life has to offer to those who are willing to take. I take so those who surround me must also, or be taken advantage of by the strong. There has been only one woman who has ever captured my full attention but we can never be. So all I have to look forward to is the conquest of my world. Damn, I never envisioned myself as a man without the ambition to love but that has come to past to last forever.

The Last Ride

I have awakened from my deep sleep to take control of my kingdom once again. I lost so many men in my last campaign it would be foolish to name them all. May the slain rest peacefully without anyone disturbing their memory. I have acquired a new team as I venture back out to find my place among the ruling families of this world. The mission has gotten harder since the last great ride of the untouchables. Eight of my generals along with myself are the last of the army. I was defeated the last time because of my inexperience and for the simple reason that I allowed my feelings to get involved. I have become incorrigible because life has been taken from me since the beginning of my existence. As I glance back on the lives of my fellow soldiers of war, I have come to the conclusion we have lived crazy lives. We have rarely allowed anything to come in between our covenant. All I have left to say to those who bear my pain and have developed the same lust of power as I is dream no more, breathe forever, and wash away your sins as the heavens part to shower the world. May we meet again and again on the battlefield of life. Damn.

When War Enters a Young Man's Life

War arrives in the lives of young men regardless
if they want it in their life.

When the chips fall one must be prepared to
accept the challenge or fall victim to the destruction
of the opposing force.

Heartache is a realistic emotion that we must
face. All of the soldiers will not return so the bond
must be strong amongst the comrades that posses
the heart of William Wallace.

They must also harness the hatred of Shaka
Zulu to drive back the ruling forces.

Democracy is not our objective; the quest for
unrivaled power is our position.

The position of supreme rule is on the mind of
the most powerful nation in the world. We are just
taking a page out of their book and placing it in
ours.

There is only one mission complete and it's total
domination of our world.

The Parting of the Heavens

The heavens have been cleared as the sky above parts to allow the sun to shine upon the inhabitants of the earth. I breathe harder everyday as I awake to gaze upon the creation produced by the master creator. I long for a place of my own away from those who want to see me gone. My faith is in a shaky state, undetermined at this point. Religion, I don't follow it at all, because none of those cults satisfy endeavors of mine. Blind, I am not, because I see the traps that men lay for those who are eager to join or belong to an organization. Driven by greed is my soul, I know this because I am willing to give it up to obtain worldly possessions. I'd rather have assets than love because love has cost me too much.

Journey for the Truth

The journey for the truth is one that will take endless nights of searching through different text and the soul.

The truth to most is what they have been told or taught over the years.

The majority of the time what one is taught is a tainted version of what the truth really is because men fabricate different truths when the time or situation arises.

I think that the truth resides within us all, but takes the back seat to what people put before it.

To see what is truly real, one must look within for the answer.

A Look through Lucifer's Eyes

I dance to the song of the devil

A rebel with God's eyes

Cursed to be looked at as insane in the minds of
most people.

My thoughts are saluted with craziness in the
pupils of those who ride.

As I collide with the obstacles in front of me,

The blitzkrieg war strategy will remove any
barrier.

Do not stand in the way of my destiny and me,

I will have no choice but to run you over.

We collide to ride – it is a do or die,

Without a scary sight my mission is to win.

The Endless War Zone

The world is a dangerous war zone full of landmines and forward areas. Men are eager to shed the blood of one another for meaningless possessions. No one truly owns anything because in death all that was previously gained is stripped from us. I, too, am a victim of what men long for... power, respect, and wealth also troubles my thoughts on a nightly basis. What I see and want is exactly what I crave. The blood of a slave runs through my veins. I have tried to wash it away, but it continues to flow regardless of what I do to dilute the mixture. Whispers of the tortured and executed excite the wind which tells their stories. For reasons unknown, I am able to hear the cries and fears of my lost peers as they relay messages through different mediums. Warning me of the trouble that awaits my every move, urging me to take a different path, because the road we have walked so far, only leads to failure. To be granted a waiver is easy, they said, "just allow the sun to shine on the path you should follow." So, I talk and walk with my favorite friends and rid myself of those who walk in a continuous direction of sin. There was a time when I was set on being the ruler of all I saw fit to rule, but I have recently found out I lack the conviction to destroy what I truly love. I hold no grudge and give no explanation. I am finished chasing something I never really needed. For the love of money, men will sell their souls, but I am no longer for sell. At one time during my life I thought it would be better to reign in hell than a servant in the kingdom of heaven. Recently, I have come to grips with what I have lost, but I still search for my inner peace. May the world always remember I am just a man, but I ask the people of the world to forget the man I once was for he no longer lives because he is now a memory in the wind.

The Last Days and Times Saga

During these last days and times, my back must be turned towards the life I once lived. I can't walk or converse in the circles I once revered. My existence out here on the streets must be plotted, scripted to a T. As I say farewell to the mismanagement of that past life, I ask the Lord to guide my new path. Without faith I might lose my drive to stay free. Running from my capture is a painful feeling, but I need my freedom because the struggle continuous in any condemned place. Man has stripped the world of its free will because of the laws he has put in place to destroy another man's livelihood. Once, again, I have cried the tears of my fellow peers throughout the years, and, poured out bottle after bottle on the pavement to allow the spirits to soak the ground. Now, the frown that was always present on my face has been turned upside down forever. Love resides deep within but devilish thoughts leak out of my mind to ravish the world. I lack the patience to deal with idiots and idol fools who stand around and just talk about things all the time. They never take the initiative to go out and pursue exactly what they want. I, too, once possessed those characteristics, but I have shed them as a snake sheds its skin in preparation to display a new. My new view of the world is a blessing, yes, a blessing. If my eyes had not been opened to the horrors of life, I probably would still be submerged in my poisonous former life.

Shadows are the Key

Shadows posses the answers to questions that puzzle the minds of men. Even though hope is present in the thought process of those who want for a better life, the idea will not materialize until the steps are taken to secure that sought after position. I was born on April 4, during the year of 1980, in the midst of the cocaine revolution, which I think destroyed so many great minds. But that era also opened up the eyes of the eager beaver willing to surrender his life for a greater purpose.

Nevertheless, my fate has been placed in my own hands after the mathematical equation has been put in motion. The gathering of militant-minded revolutionaries has begun, no cowards allowed, we've drawn our ambitions in buckets of hate for the love of power. I tower above dummies and fools in the war that we choose to wage within the slums that we have created. Sometimes, we feel as though there must be a better way, but the mean streak that resides within our souls calls for action. After the smoke clears, the thoughts that have driven me crazy are still lurking in my mind. Fight until the night is close to an end, we are destine to be overachievers.

Starving the Mind

The malnutrition of the mind blinds the vision of those who do not seek out knowledge. Verbal abuse crushes the hopes and dreams of the person on the other end of the conversation. Laughter engulfs the world but my picture is blurry. I am looking at life through the wrong focal lens. My lens is broken, full of imperfections. Pressure is overwhelming in my circle of compadres. If one of us can find the way out, all we ask is that they extend a hand, but we must be willing to grab it and not look back. The sights I have seen throughout my life bear the pain of the lost and the living. Brother, you must be my guardian because only you can point out the flaws within my soul. Rape this world for what it has to offer and discard the rest. Bleed until there is no blood left in your body. May all the imperfection be released leaving you clean and holy. Fantasize about us united as one single group in high pursuit of one thing. Help me remove my lust for the wrong things so I can focus that lust on the agenda in our grasp.

My Vision

Through my eyes I have seen hate materialize in different capacities. If I breed, will my seed harness my hate along with their own? Who knows the answer, but hate is forever present because men continue to breathe. Do not follow me, run on an even playing field with me, as I develop myself into a man who asks for nothing, but has something to offer to those who want it. How long has the thought been present within the conscious of men who ravel through the years of life searching for a Savior that has always been there from the beginning? Dying does not scare me as much as living does because death is the full circle point of our existence. I want to reside in place of sanity not mayhem. Damn, is there a place for us who walk the thin line of righteousness when our time is over? I believe so, because we are the real people who fight to survive the coldness of the weather blown in our direction.

Memories

Memories of my father haunt my sleep

He moved in and out the door on a nightly
interval

It has to be away to get out of this predicament
I have placed myself in

But my surrogate father's blood rushes through
my veins

Somewhere in between the worlds of murder,
mayhem, and greed I have found the lost plan

The line of love and hate has been crossed by so
many

I have learned to ignore the recurring dream but
the memories linger on

So many say that they can remember but I know
I will never forget the troubling thoughts that are
present within

I will never cry again.

The Flow of Prosperity

Maintain the flow of prosperity so that we can continue to control our agenda. Open up the doors that have been locked for so long. As my eyes part in the morning, grant me pardon from my sins. I know I've done a lot to undo what was created beyond my power. Please, answer my plea for forgiveness or show me the way to obtain peace of mind. The tale has been written, my hopeless whispers lead to the answers read during my conviction. I do not know what the verdict reads but I hope my plea will be answered. I beg to be free, to see the fruits of my labor materialize. I am lost and turned away to present my case another day. I have failed more than once and will fall flat on my face again. Believe me, I am just a small part of the big puzzle that is not yet fully assembled. Don't turn me away, let me in for I have seen the vision come to past and this time it ends.

From the Heights of the Heavens and the Depths of Hell

For the love of money, men will sell their souls. It is kind of funny, because what we crave cannot be bought. Happiness is within the eye of the beholder. The fallen angels have risen again to befriend the troubled souls of men. As we say farewell to the sky and hello to the inferno of everlasting flames, there will be no change in the thought process of the caged beast. My feast has been placed in front of my face to be devoured in a timely manner. As the great Charlemagne once did in his quest to conquer his world, we must also unify our collective thoughts for the reckoning. I believe the key to achieving one's goals is to have faith in the higher power. The importance of being a believer speaks for itself. The hustler within me dreams of peace and serenity, but life does not offer it to me. Help me or release me from the chains of mortality.

What Must Be Done

Are you ready to do what must be done to reign supreme over those who oppose? My focus is keen, the dream is unrivaled power. The hour hand on the clock moves slowly but the second hand moves swiftly. Murder, mayhem, and greed is what I lust for regardless of the score, I have just begun my tour of war. I am away from all those I love except the men who collide and fight with me. Remember that we must do what has to be done to finish first. If the goals we have set for ourselves are not achieved then we have failed one another. The absence of our fathers in our lives has dealt us a bad start. The memories of the pain, which has stuck with each individual, helped develop the fire within us all. From the beginning to the end of our stint on this earth, what one cherishes is what one uses to determine his or her self-worth. Youthful aspiration to oversee the flow of currency has derailed so many dreams and spelled out danger. Will someone please show me the way to control this vengeful nature, so I can hold on to my life as a free man?

Introduction

I can't run from the man I am anymore. Mediocrity is not my fate in the land that holds endless amounts of opportunity for one to take advantage of. By trying not to hurt the feelings of those who claim to love me, I am hurting myself by not pursuing the wealth that is in front of my face. The man that I am holds the key to unlock the world of prosperity. Show some faith in the future and drive out of the past leaving all old things behind. Today, I have taken on a new identity willing to approach all problems with apathy. As knight takes bishop, I take control of myself, never to relinquish the essence of my presence to the other side again. To look at the world through sober eyes is a blessing after a ten-year binge in the direction of self-destruction. I am only twenty-three years of age, which means that I am still a baby, but I have seen the horrors of life ten-fold.